Evaluating Future U.S. Army Force Posture in Europe

Phase I Report

PROJECT DIRECTORS
Kathleen H. Hicks
Heather A. Conley

CONTRIBUTING AUTHORS
Lisa Sawyer Samp
Olga Oliker
John O'Grady
Jeffrey Rathke
Melissa Dalton
Anthony Bell

February 2016

CSIS | CENTER FOR STRATEGIC &
INTERNATIONAL STUDIES

ROWMAN &
LITTLEFIELD

Lanham • Boulder • New York • London

About CSIS

For over 50 years, the Center for Strategic and International Studies (CSIS) has worked to develop solutions to the world's greatest policy challenges. Today, CSIS scholars are providing strategic insights and bipartisan policy solutions to help decisionmakers chart a course toward a better world.

CSIS is a nonprofit organization headquartered in Washington, D.C. The Center's 220 full-time staff and large network of affiliated scholars conduct research and analysis and develop policy initiatives that look into the future and anticipate change.

Founded at the height of the Cold War by David M. Abshire and Admiral Arleigh Burke, CSIS was dedicated to finding ways to sustain American prominence and prosperity as a force for good in the world. Since 1962, CSIS has become one of the world's preeminent international institutions focused on defense and security; regional stability; and transnational challenges ranging from energy and climate to global health and economic integration.

Thomas J. Pritzker was named chairman of the CSIS Board of Trustees in November 2015. Former U.S. deputy secretary of defense John J. Hamre has served as the Center's president and chief executive officer since 2000.

CSIS does not take specific policy positions; accordingly, all views expressed herein should be understood to be solely those of the author(s).

ISBN: 978-1-4422-5924-9 (pb); 978-1-4422-5925-6 (eBook)

Center for Strategic & International Studies
1616 Rhode Island Avenue, NW
Washington, DC 20036
202-887-0200 | www.csis.org

Rowman & Littlefield
4501 Forbes Boulevard
Lanham, MD 20706
301-459-3366 | www.rowman.com

Contents

Acknowledgments

This project would not have been possible without the combined efforts of the International Security Program, the Europe Program, and the Russia and Eurasia Program at CSIS. The project's principal investigators, Kathleen Hicks and Heather Conley, thank the many experts and staff throughout CSIS who contributed to the study, beginning with Olga Oliker and Lisa Sawyer Samp, and including Mark Cancian, Jeffrey Rathke, Melissa Dalton, COL John O'Grady (USA), Jeffrey Mankoff, James Mina, and Anthony Bell.

This material is based upon work supported by the U.S. Army Europe under contract number HQ0034-12-A-0022-0012. Any opinions, findings, and conclusions or recommendations expressed in this material are those of the authors and do not necessarily reflect the view of the U.S. Army Europe.

CSIS thanks U.S. Army Europe for their support in conducting this review. In addition, the study team would like to thank officials in the Office of the Secretary of Defense, the Army Staff, the Joint Staff, the Department of State, and the National Security Council who provided valuable time and insights for this review. In addition to those within the U.S. government, CSIS consulted with many nongovernmental experts in Washington and in Europe. Their insights and perspectives informed the report's findings and analysis.

While the findings of this report remain those of the authors, this study would not have been possible without the contributions of all those listed above.

Evaluating Future U.S. Army Force Posture in Europe

Introduction

Russia's violations of Ukrainian sovereignty—illegally annexing Crimea in early 2014, and its ongoing military support to separatist rebels in eastern Ukraine—as well as its continued violation of Georgian sovereignty, repeated challenges to the Intermediate Nuclear Forces (INF) Treaty, and withdrawal from the Conventional Forces in Europe (CFE) Treaty challenge the most basic assumptions of Europe's security. Amid these heightened tensions, Moscow has conducted large snap military exercises along NATO's eastern and northern border and has expanded its naval and air patrols along the periphery of NATO territory. Moreover, the Russian military intervention in Syria in September 2015 underscores Russia's increasing willingness to use military force to advance its interests, which culminated in the November 24, 2015, shoot-down of a Russian SU-24 aircraft by NATO member Turkey. These destabilizing acts threaten the abiding U.S. interest in the security of Europe—to which the United States is bound by treaty obligation—including extensive trade and investment ties and decades of close foreign policy partnership.

With this in mind, such a dramatic shift in both the European and transatlantic security paradigm requires a reevaluation of a full range of measures required for the United States to best deter Russia from similar acts of adventurism in and around alliance territory. In support of this reevaluation and to identify the appropriate role for U.S. Army Europe in a twenty-first century deterrence strategy, this report reviews Russian capabilities and forces; considers alternative U.S. force posture arrangements; assesses how to determine whether assurance and deterrence goals are being met; and identifies concrete budget recommendations in order to optimize the U.S. Army's presence in Europe.

Scope and Objectives

Commissioned by U.S. Army Europe (USAREUR), this report represents the first of a two-phase review by CSIS of USAREUR force posture in light of the substantial changes to the European security environment. It lays out the elements of a deterrence strategy toward Russia and offers specific initiatives for consideration in the Department of Defense's (DoD) FY 2017 budget request. The CSIS study team conducted the first phase of this analysis between September 30 and December 30, 2015. As part of this phase, CSIS sought to determine the following: what is needed from the U.S. Army to contribute to deterring Russia in both the near and mid-terms; the degree to which U.S. Army posture and assistance methods affect deterrence goals; how U.S. Army leaders and others can best understand whether deterrence goals are being met by identifying metrics to evaluate progress; and what specific initiatives would have the most impact on advancing U.S. deterrence goals. To facilitate this analysis, the CSIS study team reviewed existing literature, undertook original analysis, and conducted interviews with senior officials from U.S. Army, U.S. European Command (USEUCOM), the Office of the Secretary of Defense, Joint Staff, Congress, NATO allies, and think tank experts.

Russian Military Context

In Ukraine and Georgia, Russia has demonstrated its willingness to use military force for territorial and political gains, and President Vladimir Putin has shown an increasing readiness to take significant risks. Russia's current military posture and size; its application of the 2014 Russian military doctrine; and its anti-access/area denial (A2/AD) posture create a dilemma for the United States and its NATO allies seeking to ensure the ability to deter and, if necessary, defeat future Russian aggression.

Russia divides its forces into four geographic military districts stretching from Eastern Europe to the Asia-Pacific, two of which border Europe. The Western Military District headquartered in St. Petersburg is focused on the Baltic States, Kaliningrad, and the Far North. Russian forces in this district consist of approximately 22 Battalion Tactical Groups (BTGs), which are similar in role to U.S. Brigade Combat Teams (BCTs) although somewhat smaller.[1] The Western Military District is also home to the Russian Navy's Baltic Fleet based in Kaliningrad and the Northern Fleet based in Severomorsk. The Southern Military District, currently focused on Crimea and Ukraine, contains approximately 30 BTGs.[2] The Central Military District is focused on Central Asia, while the Eastern Military District focuses on Northeast Asia. Russian forces can rapidly reposition between all four military districts in order to concentrate forces against a single point, if so ordered.

In recent years, Russia has notably increased the size and frequency of its annual military exercises, and taken additional steps such as staging snap exercises and conducting surprise inspections of military units, steps aimed to improve the combat readiness of Russian forces for large-scale regional conflicts.[3] Between February 2014 and September 2015, Russia conducted at least six snap exercises of various scope and size and two large-scale planned exercises involving forces in the Western, Central, and Southern Military Districts.[4] A snap exercise in Kaliningrad consisted of 9,000 military

[1] A Russian BTG consists of a mission command element, three combat maneuver elements of armor with additional artillery, air defense, engineer, and enablers. Phillip A. Karber, "'New Generation Warfare': Coming to a Theatre Near You?" (presentation, Lessons Learned from Russo-Ukraine, Gloucestershire, UK, Innsworth, October 30, 2015).

[2] "Chapter Five: Russia and Eurasia,' in *Military Balance*, 1st ed., vol. 115 (London: International Institute for Strategic Studies, 2015), 191–95.

[3] See Johan Norberg, *Training to Fight—Russia's Major Military Exercises 2011–2014*, FOI-R-4128-SE (Stockholm, FOI, December 2015), http://www.foi.se/sv/Sok/Sammanfattningssida/?rNo=FOI-R--4128--SE.

[4] Russia has conducted at least 18 snap exercises in the past three years. Jens Stoltenberg, "Modernising the Rule-book of European Security," North Atlantic Treaty Organization, November 26, 2015, http://www.nato.int/cps/en/natohq/opinions_125177.htm. See also Ian J. Brzezinski and Nicholas Varangis, "The NATO-Russia Exercise Gap," Atlantic Council, February 23, 2015, http://www.atlanticcouncil.org/blogs/natosource/the-nato-russia-exercise-gap; Anna Maria Dyner, "Russian Military Exercises: Preparation for Expeditionary Operations," Polish Institute of International Affairs, *Bulletin* No. 86 (818), September 25,

personnel, along with hundreds of armored vehicles and artillery.[5] Another snap exercise in the Western and Central Military Districts mobilized 150,000 personnel and the Baltic Fleet. These exercises demonstrate Moscow's ability to rapidly move military forces along its borders and pose an immediate concern to NATO's Eastern allies. Poland, for instance, was motivated to invoke Article 4 consultations at NATO headquarters in March 2014 given the perceived threat these exercises represented to its security.

Another significant cause for concern with regard to Russian posture is Moscow's deployment of anti-access/area denial (A2/AD)-capable systems in areas critical to U.S. and allied global and regional force projection. Russia has long-range air-defense missiles, anti-ship missiles, and surface-to-surface missiles positioned in Kaliningrad, the Arctic, Belarus, Crimea, along its own western border, and now increasingly in Syria. These give Moscow the ability to contest the critical land, sea, and air pathways to the Baltic States, the Black Sea, and elsewhere in Central and Eastern Europe. While the focus of U.S. policymakers has been on China's A2/AD capabilities in the Pacific, it is now also necessary to take into account how Russia's A2/AD posture in Europe and potentially the Middle East, create their own unique challenges. Namely, the relatively limited nature of U.S. forward-positioned capabilities in Eastern Europe, which necessitates global and regional repositioning of manpower, equipment, and materiel in the event of a contingency anywhere near Russia's western borders.

Beyond the use of conventional forces, Russia has developed an effective set of instruments and methods of coercion that are cheap to use and difficult to deter. The manner in which the Kremlin has blended various modes of warfare, political subversion, covert action, and economic pressure poses serious challenges to the United States and European allies seeking to deter further Russian military aggression and non-military aggressive behavior. Modern Russian military doctrine calls for a comprehensive approach to warfare, relying less on traditional force-on-force scenarios and more on principles of asymmetry by attacking and exploiting enemy weakness and avoiding areas of an adversary's strength. It calls for establishing favorable conditions as precursors for military operations through subversion, information operations, and cyber operations. Russia relies on ambiguity to cloak both its actions and intentions to the maximum extent possible, providing plausible deniability and ensuring actions are below NATO's Article 5 ("an attack against one is an attack against all") threshold. It seeks to avoid decisive, sustained, large-scale warfare with an equal or more capable opponent, while advancing more limited objectives if it calculates that the gains outweigh the costs. This doctrine has been put into action in Crimea and eastern Ukraine. Russia has the capability to use these same tools elsewhere and the Kremlin can pose a direct challenge to NATO insofar as Russia can operate both ambiguously and rapidly before allies can agree upon and implement a coherent and unified response. Russia has significantly refined its coercive tools, particularly in the information and

2015, https://www.pism.pl/files/?id_plik=20535. Additional information provided by U.S. Army Europe (USAREUR).
[5] "Russia Carried Out Snap Military Drills in Kaliningrad Region," Reuters, December 16, 2014, http://www.reuters.com/article/us-russia-military-drills-idUSKBN0JU0JZ20141216.

cyber operations space, since the 2008 war with Georgia, and it likely will continue to study and improve its ability to apply force to achieve military and political ends.

Extended Deterrence in Europe

In formulating a deterrence strategy toward Russia in Europe, the United States and NATO should assume that the Baltic States represent one of the most likely flashpoints between NATO and Russia. Estonia, Latvia, and Lithuania are former Soviet Republics; Estonia and Latvia continue to have sizable ethnic Russian minorities; and since regaining independence in 1991, all three joined NATO and the European Union in 2004. While most analysts do not currently judge a Russian cross-border attack on these countries as likely, the experience of Crimea and eastern Ukraine demonstrates that is far from impossible. In this context, the CSIS study team judges the most probable scenario involving Russian military aggression in the Baltic States to be a limited seizure of territory in Estonia or Latvia by "little green men" not wearing insignia and aimed at taking control of ethnic Russian enclaves along the Russian border. However, to cover the entire spectrum of possibilities, the United States and its allies must ensure that their deterrence strategy also covers the existential threat of a full-scale Russian conventional attack aimed at seizing and conquering capitals. Such actions would clearly trigger NATO's Article 5 collective-defense commitment and would require a strong response if NATO is to retain credibility.

The most important element of deterrence is the adversary's perception of the credibility of the defender's commitment. There are two essential elements of credibility: intent and capability. Intent is based on the adversary's perception that the defender *will* make good on what it says it will do. Capability refers to the adversary's perception that the defender *can* make good on its commitments.[6] Deterrence can be pursued through two avenues that seek to manipulate an adversary's cost-benefit analysis: deterrence through punishment and deterrence through denial.[7] Deterrence-by-punishment is the promise to impose punitive costs for an act of aggression sufficient to make that aggression not worth the pain. Deterrence-by-denial is the commitment to reduce the perceived benefits of aggressive action by ensuring that the aggressor cannot successfully achieve its objectives. Deterrence strategies can incorporate elements of both punishment and denial.[8]

Deterrence-by-punishment can take the form of the promise of a harsh counter-strike in the event of aggression, or of tenacious resistance, which can inflict substantial pain on the aggressor. It can also comprise non-military actions such as economic sanctions, political isolation, and reduced cooperation in other areas. The costs inflicted by these punishments are both indirect and reactive, but offer valuable deterrence if credible. For example, if Russia used military force against a NATO member, in addition to any

---

[6] Alex S. Wilner, *Deterring Rational Fanatics* (Philadelphia: University of Pennsylvania Press, 2015), 22.

[7] See Glenn H. Snyder, *Deterrence and Defense: Toward a Theory of National Security* (Princeton, NJ: Princeton University Press, 1961) 14–16.

[8] Robert Powell, *Nuclear Deterrence Theory: The Search for Credibility* (Cambridge: Cambridge University Press, 1990), 8.

potential military costs, Moscow could reasonably expect the United States and its European allies to retaliate with severe economic sanctions—orders of magnitude greater than those imposed in response to Ukraine—and diplomatic isolation. Given the importance of economic ties to Europe for an already-weakened Russian economy, such threats could act as a strong deterrent. If, however, Russian leaders perceived European and transatlantic solidarity as weak and European leaders as divided or hesitant to accept the painful impact that such sanctions would have on their own fragile economies, the deterrent value of these threats would be diminished.

Crafting a deterrence strategy requires careful attention to two components: what the defender and aggressor can bring to a potential fight (and most importantly, how quickly) and how what the defender could bring will be perceived by the aggressor in terms of raising the costs of attacking. Deterrence at its core is a form of signaling and perception, specifically the perception of the state to be deterred is more important than reality in this context. While it is impossible to predict with perfect accuracy just how states will read each other's signals, especially in the case of Russia, it is possible to craft a strategy that signals as clearly as possible both capability and credibility. Here force posture is critical.

Force posture includes both the forces needed to demonstrate capability and intent, and the ways one is threatening to use these forces. For states that possess nuclear weapons, deterrence can be divided into nuclear deterrence and conventional deterrence.[9] Nuclear deterrence implies a threat of nuclear weapon use, tactical or strategic. This is almost always deterrence-by-punishment. Even if their use also precludes attainment of the military objective, the destructive power of available nuclear weapons and the high risks of nuclear retaliation imply a willingness to do a tremendous amount of damage to the adversary and sustain a very high level of damage oneself. Years of non-use of nuclear weapons also create an environment in which nuclear use is perceived as reckless, crossing a threshold that there is worldwide agreement not to cross.

During the Cold War, NATO's deterrence strategy against the Soviet Union's conventional superiority in Europe relied on the threat of nuclear punishment to deter a Soviet conventional attack.[10] While the United States, France, and the United Kingdom retain substantial nuclear capabilities and NATO is currently reexamining its nuclear doctrine, the alliance today cannot reasonably rely on nuclear threats alone to deter Russian aggression in the Baltic States, particularly if Moscow were to pursue such aggression using more surreptitious methods of warfare as witnessed in Ukraine. Nuclear threats in these circumstances would lack credibility for several reasons. First, they would likely be seen as a disproportionate response to Russian unconventional or conventional action.

[9] See John J. Mearsheimer, *Conventional Deterrence* (Ithaca, NY: Cornell University Press, 1983); Michael Gerson, "Conventional Deterrence in the Second Nuclear Age," *Parameters* 39, no. 3 (2009): 32–48; John C. Hopkins and Steven A. Maaranen, "Nuclear Weapons in Post-Cold War Deterrence," in *Post-Cold War Conflict Deterrence*, by Naval Studies Board (Washington, DC: National Academies Press, 1997), 115–19.
[10] U.S. forces in Western Europe served as a tripwire for the U.S. nuclear response to assure European allies that Washington would retaliate on their behalf and deter the Soviet Union from acting on its conventional advantage.

NATO has substantial conventional capabilities at its disposal and it is difficult to believe it would escalate to nuclear use without first trying an alternative strategy. Second, the risks of escalation are high, and NATO unity would be difficult to maintain. Thus, nuclear weapons offer limited deterrence value in the immediate context of the Russian actions as against the Baltic States that are postulated above. Given the limited credibility of nuclear threats, the United States must rely upon non-nuclear military forces, alongside economic and other diplomatic tools, as the primary means of deterring Russian aggression.

It is also important that the 1997 non-legally binding political agreement, the Founding Act on Mutual Relations, Cooperation and Security (NATO-Russia Founding Act, or NRFA), was agreed to by NATO allies and Russia, stating that:

> In the current and foreseeable security environment, the Alliance will carry out its collective defense and other missions by ensuring the necessary interoperability, integration, and capability for reinforcement rather than by *additional permanent stationing of substantial combat forces.* Accordingly, it will have to rely on adequate infrastructure commensurate with the above tasks. In this context, reinforcement may take place, when necessary, in the event of defense against a threat of aggression and missions in support of peace consistent with the United Nations Charter and the OSCE [Organization for Security and Cooperation in Europe] governing principles, as well as for exercises consistent with the adapted CFE [Conventional Armed Forces in Europe] Treaty, the provisions of the Vienna Document 1994 and mutually agreed transparency measures. Russia will exercise similar restraint in its conventional force deployments in Europe [emphasis added].[11]

Because infrastructure and reinforcements are explicitly permitted by the Founding Act, an increase in U.S. or alliance forces or prepositioned stocks would not require the NRFA to be revisited. Although it was never stipulated what qualifies as a "substantial" force increase, U.S. and allied policymakers will need to develop a common position on this issue. To date, there is no agreement within the alliance to no longer abide by the NRFA.

Crafting the ground forces component of an effective strategy of extended deterrence in Europe is complicated by a number of factors, mostly related to the size and expenditure involved in maintaining large numbers of conventional forces in Europe during peacetime. First, U.S. Army personnel permanently stationed in Europe have steadily declined from roughly 200,000 during the 1980s to approximately 33,000 in 2015.[12] At the height of the Cold War, the United States had two U.S. Army Corps with heavy armored

---

[11] *Founding Act on Mutual Relations, Cooperation and Security between NATO and the Russian Federation,* NATO-Russia, May 27, 1997, NATO, http://www.nato.int/cps/en/natohq/official_texts_25468.htm.
[12] Data on USAREUR personnel strength from 1945–1991 provided by USAREUR Historian's Office, Heidelberg, Germany, found in Ingo Wolfgang Trauschweizer, "Creating Deterrence for Limited War: The U.S. Army and the Defense of West Germany, 1953–1982" (PhD diss., University of Maryland, 2006), 417, http://drum.lib.umd.edu/handle/1903/3390.

forces and all the associated enablers to conduct sustained land combat.[13] Today, the United States has only two permanently stationed Brigade Combat Teams, the Army's baseline deployable combat unit consisting of approximately 4,000 troops, in Europe.[14] It has also closed a significant amount of its ground forces infrastructure (over 100 sites since 2006); removed much of its heavy equipment from the continent; and concentrated its remaining forces in several locations in western Germany and Italy. The $1 billion European Reassurance Initiative (ERI), begun in response to Russia's 2014 annexation of Crimea, helped to increase the capability of USAREUR, notably with the addition of a rotational Armored Brigade Combat Team (ABCT) to Europe, although these measures are currently funded on a temporary basis.

Second, as the threat of conventional warfare in Europe diminished, the key lens through which U.S. ground forces have engaged allies has been theater security cooperation (TSC) activities to improve allies' expeditionary capabilities for use in Iraq and Afghanistan. As such, U.S. and allied militaries have not maintained a high level of readiness to defend territory in Europe. Today, U.S. TSC activities with host nations in the Baltic States and Eastern Europe have generally been small-scale, using company-sized elements across nine countries at a time.

Third, two decades of enlarging the alliance has shifted its borders hundreds of miles eastward from central Germany to the Baltic States, Poland, Bulgaria, and Romania. Alliance infrastructure, however, has remained largely in Germany and Western Europe. The bulk of U.S. and NATO forces, which enjoy overall numerical and technological superiority over Russian forces, are not currently positioned to serve as forward forces on a day-to-day basis along NATO's eastern flank, complicating their ability to extend a credible deterrence-by-denial threat. Russia, on the other hand, maintains superiority in the local military balance across NATO's entire eastern flank, home to some of the alliance's least-modern and least-capable militaries. Thus, the local military balance in the Baltic region is tilted heavily in Moscow's favor. Estonia, Latvia, and Lithuania can field approximately 10,000 active-duty soldiers collectively, with virtually no air or naval capabilities.[15]

Finally, public finances in the United States and European states are under intense pressure and most governments and parliaments have resisted increases to their country's defense spending. Despite calls from U.S. and NATO leaders for allies to better share the burden of defense, the gap in spending has continued to widen; the United States now contributes approximately 73 percent of aggregate alliance defense spending while representing only 50 percent of aggregate alliance GDP.[16] At the September 2014

---

[13] "Enablers" refers to mission command, intelligence, artillery, aviation, engineers, and sustainment.
[14] These units are the 173rd Airborne Brigade Combat Team based in Vicenza, Italy, and the 2nd Cavalry Regiment based in Vilseck, Germany.
[15] See "Chapter Four: Europe," in *Military Balance*, 1st ed., vol. 115 (London: International Institute for Strategic Studies, 2015).
[16] North Atlantic Treaty Organization, Public Diplomacy Division, "Financial and Economic Data Relating to NATO Defence," June 22, 2015, NATO, http://www.nato.int/nato_static_fl2014/assets/pdf/pdf_2015_06/20150622_PR_CP_2015_093-v2.pdf.

NATO Summit in Wales, allied leaders agreed to halt any further defense cuts and gradually move toward NATO's defense spending benchmark of 2 percent of GDP within the next decade. While the decline has been arrested, progress on increasing spending, however, has been slow alliance-wide, regardless of significant shifts in the European security landscape. In contrast, Russia, the world's third-largest defense spender, has increased its real defense spending by $20 billion since 2013. Despite economic woes, Russia is entering the sixth year of an ambitious 10-year military modernization program that aims to spend over $700 billion upgrading Russian military equipment, with approximately $436 billion already spent.[17]

Military Capabilities for Conventional Deterrence

The capabilities for deterrence are distinct from the capabilities needed to conduct an active defense against aggression if deterrence were to fail. The latter is critical to both deterrence-by-denial and deterrence-by-punishment, of course, but a variety of other factors go in to signaling credibility as well as capability. Specifically, naval and air power have important roles to play in an active defense of the Baltic States, are crucial to the projection of U.S. military power in Europe, and possess a variety of capabilities that Russian planners have been concerned about for decades. Moreover, Russian military exercises in the theater have further demonstrated the complex interplay between air-land-naval forces in the Baltic region. Therefore, the importance of air and naval components to deterrence cannot be ignored. However, ground forces bring something to the table that the others cannot: the immediacy and continuous nature of their presence and their ability to physically block the advance of an adversary's ground forces in the event of an invasion.[18] In short, ground forces are far more difficult for an adversary to discount because they are often physically in the way.

This is not to suggest, however, that more ground forces equate to stronger deterrence in and of themselves. Deterrence emphasizes forces that are: visible in that the adversary knows they will be a threat and must account for their presence; flexible in terms of having the speed to react and adapt to different circumstances; and expandable in terms of their ability to be rapidly strengthened through reinforcement. Conventional forces can be described as falling within one of three roles: forward forces; rapid-response forces; and follow-on forces. The distinction between these roles rests in the forces' proximity to the adversary's objectives at the time of the attack and the amount of time the adversary perceives it would take for forces to deploy into the field in relation to the adversary's timetable for achieving its goals. Therefore, it is possible for the United States to significantly increase the size of its conventional forces in Germany and Italy but gain little deterrence value if these forces do not possess the right mix of capabilities and presence to factor into Moscow's calculus regarding the Baltic States. Similarly, multinational forces, while they might have less cohesion than a purely national force, have the benefit of conveying broader political commitment and could potentially have a

---

[17] "Chapter Five: Russia and Eurasia," in *Military Balance*, 1st ed., vol. 115 (London: International Institute for Strategic Studies, 2015), 164.
[18] This paper assumes U.S. Navy, Air Force, and Marine Corps forces in Europe remain constant.

greater deterrent effect since the adversary would need to contemplate entering hostilities against more than one opponent.

Forward Forces

Forward forces can deny an adversary freedom of action and raise the risks of aggression.[19] In terms of posture and capabilities, they can either be permanently or rotationally deployed with either light or heavy forces. Forward-deployed forces signal a high level of political and military commitment to both allies and adversaries and have the potential to offer a higher degree of deterrence value than rapid-response and follow-on forces due to their immediate and continuous presence. Such forces amount to a "tripwire" that would trigger broader U.S. military involvement. They can also present a substantial threat of punishment to any forces that come into contact with them. Presence alone, however, is not necessarily a credible deterrent. Forward-deployed forces must, therefore, meet several conditions in order to offer an effective minimum deterrent.

First, these forces must possess some relevant combat capability to ensure a punishment component and to underline credibility. Otherwise, an adversary may discount them. Forces that cannot fight cannot deter. As previously mentioned, U.S. forces currently deploying to the Baltic States are generally oriented toward security cooperation and may not possess sufficient equipment and munitions to serve as deterrent forces.

Second, there should not be periods of time in which forward-deployed forces are absent so that an adversary cannot hope to avoid an encounter. U.S. forward-deployed forces in the Baltic States are rotational forces that stay for several months at a time, often with gaps of time in which no U.S. forces are present. While rotational forces can provide a forward-deployed presence for deterrence, rotations must be timed so as not to offer an adversary an open window for aggression.[20]

Third, these forces must be appropriately sized and positioned so as to be capable of tripping the escalatory threshold for greater U.S. involvement. A force that is too small can be avoided and presents the aggressor with the prospect of achieving its objectives without risking escalation. Determining the right size and positions for forward forces will be difficult in situations where the aggressor's goals are limited and highly localized, a hallmark of Russian ambiguous warfare.

Rapid-Response Forces

Rapid-response forces emphasize high mobility. As such, they may sacrifice some combat power, but they can possess high deterrence value by denying an adversary a quick and

---

[19] For a discussion on conventional capabilities in deterrence, see Kenneth Watman, Dean Wilkening, John Arquilla, and Brian Nichiporuk, *U.S. Regional Deterrence Strategies* (Santa Monica, CA: RAND Corporation, 1995), 84–86.

[20] The frequent rotation of forces with different capabilities may possess some deterrence value by introducing greater uncertainty into the adversary's plans.

decisive victory. These forces tend to be composed of lightly equipped forces such as light infantry, airborne infantry, air assault infantry, and special operations forces. Unlike forward forces, however, rapid-response forces require a political decision to deploy and sufficient time to marshal, transit, and take the field. Because rapid-response forces emphasize speed over combat power, policymakers face a difficult decision as to whether to actually employ forces that can be overrun by a more powerful enemy. Thus, their effectiveness as a deterrent is weakened if Russia has reason to doubt the West's willingness to commit these forces in the event of a crisis, or if Russia believes it can achieve its objectives before rapid-response forces could arrive.[21]

In recent years, NATO has turned toward multinational rapid-response forces in the shape of the NATO Response Forces (NRF), including the newly established Very High Readiness Joint Task Force (VJTF), or "spearhead force." Multinational rapid-response forces possess greater political value and achieve economies-of-scale by merging contributions from multiple states. They can thus achieve greater deterrence value by threatening to entangle the aggressor with more than one state, or NATO as a whole. Yet the deterrence value of multinational early-response forces can be diluted by a number of factors. Multinational forces by nature increase the number of stakeholders, which complicates and inevitably slows the decisionmaking process in a situation where speed is the most critical factor. At the present moment, allied leaders are resisting giving greater command-and-control authority to military leaders in anticipation of escalatory decisionmaking. In the event of inter-alliance disagreements amid a rapidly unfolding crisis, the dissent or hesitation of one ally could halt or undermine the ability of the alliance or individual states to promptly respond.

Follow-On Forces

Follow-on forces are stationed in rear areas that must be mobilized. They generally possess significant war-fighting capability but low deterrence value because they are the slowest to arrive to the battlefield. While moving military personnel across continents and within theaters is relatively quick and cheap, it is the transportation of large volumes of heavy equipment that is the most difficult obstacle. Prepositioning equipment forward can accelerate the timetables for the deployment of follow-on forces and therefore increase their deterrent value.

In the context of the Baltic States, the United States would likely rely on two waves of follow-on forces. The first wave would include the deployment of the permanent or rotational forces in Europe and troops from the United States, which could fall-in on forward-deployed equipment stockpiles. The deployment timelines for these forces could range from a matter of days to over a week depending on the location of troops, the location and types of equipment, and the time for the unit to transit to the front. The second wave of follow-on forces would entail the transportation of combat forces, including troops and equipment, from the continental United States to Europe. Given that NATO's predominant advantage is conventional follow-on forces (despite existing

---

[21] Kenneth Watman, Dean Wilkening, John Arquilla, and Brian Nichiporuk, *U.S. Regional Deterrence Strategies* (Santa Monica, CA: RAND Corporation, 1995), 69.

infrastructure and political obstacles to facilitate country transit), Russia would most likely seek a quick and decisive campaign to leverage its advantage in proximity.

Enhanced Deterrence in Europe

In determining how much is enough to deter and defend, the conflict in Ukraine and U.S. military planning doctrine are instructive. A variety of factors led to the Kremlin's decision to halt further advances into eastern Ukraine. These include economic sanctions and diplomatic engagement as well as the poor results that Russia's tactics showed as Russian and separatist forces moved further into Ukraine (particularly in Odessa and Mariupol). At the same time, stronger-than-anticipated local and Ukrainian military resistance certainly had an impact. Based on the experience in Crimea, Russia likely expected little in the way of effective armed resistance in eastern Ukraine. Initially, it seemed to have been proven right. But from January 2014 to May 2014, Ukraine executed the largest single military mobilization to counter a threat in Europe since World War II, deploying 15 to 20 brigades to the country's east. Ukraine's mass mobilization generated sufficient force ratios of about 1:3 to defend against Russian and separatist forces. This is consistent with a general principle in military planning that states that defending forces in possession of a 1:3 force ratio can hold attacking forces to a 65–75 percent chance of success. In other words, attacking forces will retain a reasonable chance of success, but at a higher cost and in a manner unlikely to be quick and decisive.[22] After Ukraine had mobilized its forces, Russia then increased its own involvement, making it more difficult to credibly deny its military presence, but it also confined its military actions to the vicinity of territory it already controlled. This experience offers a starting point when considering the additional U.S. and allied forces required to affect Putin's calculus.

In order to offer a credible deterrent against Russian aggression in the Baltic States, the CSIS study team recommends a strategy based on a tiered and scalable posture for U.S. Army forces in Europe. This approach would allow U.S. and allied forces to establish a strong tripwire in the Baltic States and quickly expand to provide forward forces, rapid-response forces, and initial echelons of follow-on forces nearing the 1:3 force ratio, with the ability to scale up further if Russia escalates.

To be clear, this proposal outlines a strategy to deter Russian aggression against the Baltic States by establishing credible U.S. and allied capabilities for conventional deterrence in the region. It is not a strategy to conduct an active defense of the Baltic States in the event deterrence fails. The worst-case scenario is when Russia employs overwhelming military force to rapidly seize the Baltic States without having to encounter U.S. or Western military forces. In such a scenario, Moscow would be able to place the burden of escalation on Washington and Brussels, rather than Moscow having

---

[22] See Trevor Nevitt Dupuy, *Analysis of Factors That Have Influenced Outcomes of Battles and Wars: A Database of Battles and Engagements*, Vols. 1–6, Report No. CAA-SR-84-6, Prepared for U.S. Army Concepts Analysis Agency (Dunn Loring: Historical Evaluation and Research Organization, September 1984). For a discussion on the 3:1 force ratio, see John J. Mearsheimer, "Assessing the Conventional Balance: The 3:1 Rule and Its Critics," *International Security* 13, no. 4 (Spring 1989): 54–89. See also Michael E. O'Hanlon, *The Future of Land Warfare* (Washington, DC: Brookings Institution, 2015), 85.

to contend with the certainty of such an escalation in its initial calculus. The CSIS study team's proposal seeks to avoid this scenario by ensuring that any Russian decision to attack the Baltic States entails a simultaneous and conscious decision to attack forward-positioned U.S. and Western European combat forces in those countries.

This proposal provides a credible deterrent commitment and can be made possible with moderate and smart increases in three areas: prepositioned equipment; troop presence and personnel; and other critical capabilities needed to counter Russian forces. There is no equation for successful deterrence, but assuming Russia could conceivably deploy up to 40 BTGs quickly in a full-scale conventional attack against the Baltic States by combining its forces in the Western and Southern Military Districts, the West would need the capacity to quickly surge to roughly 13 BCTs to satisfy the 1:3 force ratio.[23] Further assuming that NATO allies would be able to provide at least five BCTs, with up to three coming from the Baltic States, the United States should plan for a rapid surge capacity to support eight BCTs: one BCT in the category of forward forces that are continuously rotating to the Baltic States; two BCTs in the category of rapid-response forces from those already on the continent; and five BCTs in the first echelon of follow-on forces from the United States. Because NATO forces are substantially more capable than Ukrainian mobilized forces in early 2014, and we know Russia to be aware of those capabilities (in contrast to its continuing tendency to underestimate Ukrainian capacity), we expect that this will be even more effective than it was in Ukraine.

Prepositioned Equipment: The CSIS study team recommends prepositioning sufficient equipment in Europe to **support a total of eight brigades**. In addition to the equipment already in place to support the two permanent BCTs and the one European Activity Set (EAS) for the rotational Armored Brigade Combat Team (ABCT) provided under the European Reassurance Initiative (ERI), there should be: (1) **one additional EAS** for an additional rotational armored brigade combat team, (2) **one enhanced EAS** for enabling units to allow the other two EAS to be fully combat capable against Russian forces, and (3) **four brigades' worth of war-fighting stockpiles in Army Prepositioned Stocks (APS)** to enable faster response times by follow-on forces from the United States.

Troop Presence and Personnel: The CSIS study team recommends expanding upon the initial steps undertaken with ERI by allocating an **additional rotational ABCT to Europe for a total of two ABCTs.** Two rotational ABCTs will provide USAREUR with the ability to maintain a continuous rotational presence of U.S. combat forces in and around the Baltic States and Eastern Europe without the need for permanent bases. Including the two BCTs that are permanently assigned, **this will bring the total BCT forward presence in Europe to three at any given time,** and four during periods of rotational hand-over. USAREUR will also need to **add approximately 1,000 headquarters staff** to make command and control possible for rapid-response and follow-on forces.

Other Critical Capabilities: The CSIS study team recommends that USAREUR close the critical capability gaps related to joint reception, staging, onward movement, and

---

[23] Interview with former senior U.S. military officials.

integration (JRSOI); intelligence, indicators and warnings; communications; and cyber and electronic warfare.

Prepositioned Equipment

The bedrock component of this approach begins with the equipment necessary to support eight brigades, gradually inserted across a five-year future years defense plan (FYDP). To accomplish this, a modest expansion—from one to two—of the European Activity Sets (EAS) in their current form would be required. Then, an enhanced set of EAS enabler equipment would be required to provide tactical and operational mitigation against Russian capabilities. A final component would be to augment the current war-fighting stockpiles or unit equipment sets by roughly the equivalent of four BCTs plus enabling units.[24]

The CSIS study team believes it is critical to expand the ABCT EAS construct and to place an EAS for an additional ABCT, as well as provide the necessary equipment to provide organic enablers for both sets. There are sufficient armored brigades in total to source rotational forces for a persistent presence of an ABCT and also provide for the ability to conduct preplanned surges above this level of up to two ABCTs for large-scale exercises and in the event of a crisis. Having two EAS sets provides for scalability from the current rotational ABCT with months-long gaps in its presence to a persistent presence of one ABCT and the ability to surge up to two ABCTs simultaneously.

While this full capability must be demonstrated from time to time, the very nature of the scalability takes into account Russia's escalation potential and factors of operational tempo. Additionally, a U.S. commitment on this order of magnitude may assist the United States in garnering greater commitment from other NATO members.

The CSIS study team further recommends adding additional EAS enhancement in order to provide additional qualitative elements that enable U.S. BCTs to reach their full capability. These enablers would include, but are not limited to, additional artillery, short-range air defense, engineers, heavy equipment transport, military police, military intelligence, sustainment, and signal equipment all in either battalion or company-sized activity sets. As with the other European Activity Sets, this would enable allocated forces to rotate into Europe in a scalable manner.

The final and longer-term recommendation is the need to source APS, or war-fighting stocks, for the equivalent of four brigades. These stocks are the equipment and hardware that support war plans and are stored in dispersed climate-controlled facilities. This equipment should support two ABCTs, one sustainment brigade, and one fires brigade.

---

[24] The distinction between European Activity Sets (EAS) and Army Preposition Stocks (APS) is best summarized by their intended use and how they are stored. There are other distinctions such as which command they align with, funding streams, frequency of maintenance, etc., but the primary distinctions are sufficient for this analysis. EAS is stored primarily outdoors in large motor pools—that is, military parking lots. Additionally, it is generally routinely exercised for training and exercises with partner and allied nations. APS are ideally stored in climate-controlled space, configured to support SecDef-approved operation plans (OPLANs)—analogous to a "break glass" in emergency scenario.

The Army must carefully consider where to position this equipment. Ideally, these stocks should be located closest to where they will be employed in order to both reduce further transportation costs, and enhance confidence among allied host nations of the NATO security guarantee. However, Russia's A2/AD capability could threaten material and personnel positioned far forward. On the one hand, it is desirable and prudent to have forces as far forward as possible; on the other hand is the acknowledged risk that these assets are positioned in potentially contested areas.

The APS should therefore be prepositioned in multiple sites across Germany, Belgium, and the Netherlands near existing road, rail, air, and sea distribution hubs to ensure safe disbursement of stocks while retaining the ability to rapidly mass forces in a crisis. While entailing the loss of some deterrence value, these locations also allow USAREUR to take advantage of previously closed POMCUS (Prepositioning of Materiel Configured in Unit Sets) sites.

Similarly, EAS should be dispersed ranging from company to battalion size elements with enablers. These sets should be dispersed where capability currently exists to properly store this equipment. Currently, there is one site in Lithuania, one in Romania, and two in Poland. Additional sites should be surveyed and resourced to build out the capability to have up to three EAS battalion sites in Poland and up to five EAS company sites in the Baltic States, Romania, and Bulgaria.

Additional Troop Presence and Personnel

One additional rotational ABCT for Europe is another key component of the CSIS study team recommendation. The existing rotational ABCT already in place and funded by the European Reassurance Initiative (ERI) is not continuously present as it rotates between the United States and Europe. A second ABCT will allow for a heel-to-toe (that is, continuous) presence in the Baltic States and Eastern Europe and bring to three the total BCTs on the continent at any given time. As the United States considers its longer-term force posture in Europe, it should carefully weigh the costs and benefits of a rotational allocation versus permanent assignment of troops to Europe.

To support the additional rotational forces, as well as ensure command-and-control capacity for follow-on forces *in extremis*, there is a requirement for an additional 1,000 headquarters personnel in Europe. This figure includes three primary components. First, an Army command element should be permanently assigned to Europe in order to provide effective, sustainable, mission command and continuity for operations, similar to the 1st Armored Division's tactical command post (TAC) currently forward deployed to Jordan. In Europe, this element should be sourced by the division regionally aligned to Europe—currently the 4th Infantry Division. A 90-man TAC forward deployed to Europe would provide sufficient planning and execution capability required for the command and control of the additional forces allocated and assigned to USAREUR.

Second, a composite fires brigade or division artillery headquarters, with a military intelligence company and an air and missile defense section, should be permanently deployed to provide critical command and enabling capabilities. This headquarters

would augment the division headquarters and provide operational and mission command of subordinate artillery and air defense of U.S. and NATO elements that would rotate into Europe.

Third, a modest increase in assigned personnel to the USAREUR staff is necessary to provide it the capability to execute increased missions across the spectrum as a Combined/Joint Forces Land Component Command (C/JFLCC). A C/JFLCC provides the capability to design, plan, and prepare for the execution of unified land operations that support coalition and joint force commanders. This will require a modest increase and restructuring of the USAREUR headquarters.

Capability Gaps

Joint Reception, Staging, Onward Movement, and Integration (JRSOI): U.S. military strategy rests on the assumption that it would enjoy relatively unopposed lines of communication and freedom of movement to Europe to enable rapid global and regional force projection. Yet these dynamics are fundamentally challenged in the Baltic States, where strong Russian A2/AD capabilities could greatly complicate any reinforcement of the Baltic allies by sea or air. Similarly, the land route to the Baltic States traverses a narrow corridor that can be easily pinched or fully closed by Russian forces based in Kaliningrad and Belarus. This creates a challenging problem for the United States and its allies, as Russian forces are well postured to significantly disrupt—if not prevent—the flow of follow-on U.S. and NATO forces into the region in a conflict. USAREUR currently does not have the capability to conduct JRSOI today—one the most critical capability gaps faced by the U.S. forces in Europe.

There is a lack of reliable integrated air missile defense (IAMD) systems that can defend against both surface-to-air and surface-to-surface missile strikes from the Russians. This is a critical capability overmatch that could potentially prevent the United States and its allies from flowing in additional forces in the event of a high-end conflict and protecting critical civilian and military infrastructure to include seaports, airports, and other debarkation points, APS and EAS locations, critical rail and road junctions, command-and-control nodes, power distribution facilities, troop installations, and bridges. Without the ability to efficiently conduct JRSOI, U.S. deterrence threats would be undermined in a crisis.

Another significant challenge to ensuring effective theater JRSOI is Russia's effective use of unmanned aerial systems (UAS). Russia has repeatedly demonstrated its ability to quickly link information collected from UAS feeds to direct devastating artillery strikes in Ukraine. USAREUR must improve its short-range air defense (SHORAD) capabilities with the Avenger Air Defense System, which currently only exists in specific Army National Guard units such as the units dedicated to the defense of Washington, D.C. The capability to counter UAS goes beyond the scope of SHORAD, however. Electronic warfare and cyber technologies, as well as directed energy technologies, can improve freedom of movement and force protection.

Finally, USAREUR requires engineering that enables theater-wide bridging and maneuverability. USAREUR units and those that flow in during crisis response must have the ability to simultaneously conduct river crossings at multiple locations in order to ensure redundancy and no single points of failure that would inhibit force projection within the region. This assumes that even if USAREUR possessed necessary IAMD and counter-UAS capability, Russia will be successful at prosecuting some targets, especially early in a campaign when it possesses the initiative that naturally comes with the offensive. With the removal of the 12th Combat Aviation Brigade (CAB), there is also a need to think through a long-term solution to the lack of adequate helicopter lift and mobility on the continent. Sourcing an additional CAB is relatively more difficult given maintenance and cost considerations, in addition to the current high demand for these forces globally. The Army National Guard possesses a depth of capability and capacity that could be utilized.

Intelligence and Indicators and Warnings: A second capability gap is related to limited intelligence and indicators and warnings (I&W). Commanders and staff occasionally rely on open-source media as their first indicators of Russia military action. This is potentially dangerous as such information could be subject to Russian information operations. This causes a significant challenge when considering the already-disadvantaged decisionmaking process of a 28-member alliance. There is also a lack of knowledge regarding Russian signaling behaviors that may not be ascertained via traditional intelligence means, creating the possibility that signals could be misinterpreted. NATO's inability to rapidly, clearly, and effectively attribute aggression to specific actions and actors delays as well as inhibits its initial response, particularly in an environment where external military action can be concealed behind a domestic uprising.

A reevaluation of where Europe's intelligence requirements rank is warranted and requires serious consideration for higher priority in the National Intelligence Priority Framework. The most pressing intelligence capability gaps are electronic intelligence (ELINT), communications intelligence (COMINT), and geospatial intelligence (GEOINT). Furthermore, since the end of the Cold War, expertise on Russia and in Europe has atrophied within the U.S. intelligence community, with the prioritization of counter-terrorism efforts in the Middle East and South Asia as well as activities in the Asia-Pacific region. The decline in U.S. human capital dedicated to European and Russian issues creates an imperative to actively work to restore this expertise in order to more clearly and accurately identify and understand emerging threats. Additional I&W capabilities that can integrate all-source analysis and open-source information awareness, including from social media, is also needed given the criticality of time in quickly responding to minimize Russia's advantages as the initiator.

Communications: A third category of critical vulnerability is secure, redundant, and reliable communications with sufficient bandwidth. The Russians have demonstrated the capability to conduct effective electronic warfare, including disrupting undersea fiber optic cables, eavesdropping, spoofing, jamming, and more. Communications that lack adequate resiliency, range, bandwidth, and security will have a detrimental effect on USAREUR and NATO mission command and ongoing operations. The main areas that require focus in the broader signals and communications category are secure coalition tactical communications, coalition digital communications, and an unclassified common operating picture.

Cyber and Electronic Warfare: The CSIS study team underscores the pressing need to enhance U.S. and allied cyber and electronic warfare capabilities in Europe. Weaknesses in coalition cyber capabilities are a challenge that affects every area of government and, as such, is a problem far larger than the scope of this study or USAREUR's ability to address. Russia's demonstrated capabilities in this area warrant thoughtful development of counter and protective measures. USAREUR, in collaboration with others in the U.S. government and NATO, should begin to develop measures that better exploit Russian vulnerabilities. Policymakers should consider how USAREUR, with support from U.S. Army Cyber Command, might increase capacity for collaboration with the NATO Cooperative Cyber Defence Centre of Excellence located in Estonia.

Cost Considerations for Policymakers

These recommendations are costly, both in dollars and in forces. The CSIS study team acknowledges it had the luxury of assessing needed changes to U.S. Army force posture without the need to weigh the costs against other security issues facing the United States. Although the study team did not apply cost constraints to its approach, it was mindful of the financial and force burden facing the United States. The CSIS team thus incorporated a burden-sharing approach, which is critical in order to garner congressional support and to invest European allies in their own defense. Moreover, the study team's use of a strict 1:3 force ratio was an attempt to acknowledge the extreme difficulty in fully negating the local Russian force capacity advantage.

While conventional deterrence does require considerable financial support, it is far less costly by any metric than going to war with Russia. Additionally, the signaling of U.S. intent to undertake such measures, coupled with initial steps for implementation, allow the United States to lead an effort to garner necessary contributions from NATO allies such that responsibility and burden for deterrence does not fall solely on the United States. Beyond the initial cost associated with military hardware and equipment, additional costs will be incurred related primarily to military pay and allowances associated with the increase in assigned and allocated forces, operation and maintenance for additional equipment, and military construction (MILCON).

Related to MILCON, previously occupied garrisons, of which there were 41 in 1989, have been turned over to host nations or shuttered as part of the European Infrastructure Consolidation (EIC) project and are no longer available for use by U.S. forces. There remain approximately seven garrisons today, primarily located in Germany. Policymakers would be wise to reconsider this program and direct a holistic assessment, in concert with allies, of European infrastructure given the requirements of a new security environment. Other sites that are still owned but have not been used to full capacity require extensive repairs. Furthermore, sites in Eastern and Central Europe are likely to require more work to bring them up to today's standards—including upgrades to meet environmental standards, improvements to storage facilities (fuel, ammunition, petroleum products, etc.), and improvements to rail, road, and airfield infrastructure.

The equipment sets will also require routine maintenance. The frequency varies based in large part on usage rates. Naturally, the regular use of the EAS sets will require more frequent maintenance, while the APS equipment will reside in climate-controlled storage facilities and are on a fixed maintenance schedule under management of the Army Material Command (AMC).

Additional cost considerations must also be made for personnel. The CSIS study team advocates for broad use of multicomponent forces and scalability; therefore, the personnel estimate will have the greater likelihood for variance.

Ultimately, the CSIS study team judged that the cost of a credible deterrent is the price of upholding peace, which is dwarfed by the costs of war. The recent conflicts in Afghanistan and Iraq have cost upwards of $1.6 trillion. In terms of large-scale conventional conflicts, the Korean War is estimated to have cost $360 billion from 1950–53, while the Persian Gulf War from 1990–91 cost approximately $108 billion.[25] These figures also do not take into account the human and societal costs of these wars. It is safe to assume a direct conflict between the United States and Russia in Europe would be even more expensive.

Measuring Progress

Measuring the effectiveness of influence strategies such as assurance and deterrence is inherently difficult because they are based on perceptions in the minds of leaders rather than defined and clearly recognizable end states. It is a challenging proposition to attempt to determine, let alone measure, whether U.S. allies feel adequately safe under NATO's Article 5 security guarantee, or how the costs of aggression against a NATO member weigh on Russian President Vladimir Putin's mind. Even in instances where variables appear more concrete and measurable, such as evaluating the balance of military forces, quantitative measures can often paint a misleading picture of combat capabilities and effectiveness. As deterrence threats are intended to prevent an event from transpiring in the first place, it is difficult for policymakers and scholars to assess when deterrence commitments are succeeding in averting a threat or when those commitments have become genuinely unnecessary. Moreover, it is difficult for the defender to gauge the level of intent and resolve of the adversary in order to determine how potent and credible its deterrence commitments need to be.

This section, therefore, offers ideas for how the U.S. Army and others can take a comprehensive and balanced approach to understanding and communicating whether

---

[25] Cost figures adjusted to 2015 dollars. Stephen Daggett, *Cost of Major U.S. Wars*, RS22926 (Washington, DC: Congressional Research Service, June 2010), 2, https://www.fas.org/sgp/crs/natsec/RS22926.pdf; Amy Belasco, *The Cost of Iraq, Afghanistan, and Other Global War on Terror Operations Since 9/11*, RL33110 (Washington, DC: Congressional Research Service, December 2014), 1, https://www.fas.org/sgp/crs/natsec/RL33110.pdf.

assurance and deterrence policy goals are being met. Such an approach endeavors to capture both easily known statistics, such as troop numbers, alongside more intangible considerations, such as demonstrating U.S. global leadership or reinforcing the U.S. image as a dependable ally and partner, which may be difficult to measure but should not be discounted.

A useful model is one that compels its users to capture all possible quantitative and qualitative metrics and organize them into distinct, digestible, and mutually exclusive categories that can then be combined to present a fair measure of the strategic impacts of an increased focus on and investment in European security (see Figure 1). Applying such a methodical evaluation will assist policymakers, legislators, and appropriators to understand, for example, the return on investment of $1 billion in ERI funds that have been expended. The broad framework offered below is applicable not only to U.S. Army efforts, but to the full spectrum of U.S. government assurance and deterrence measures, including hard power (e.g., military actions) and soft power (e.g., economic sanctions). Thus, an analysis of the Army's efforts using this model can be easily overlaid with statistics from other DoD components in order to reach a comprehensive view of the impact of U.S. military efforts.

The CSIS study team developed a matrix that is divided into four categories covering internal, external, quantitative, and qualitative fields, and categorized as seen below into **U.S. and allied actions** (internal/quantitative), **Russian responses** (external/quantitative), **U.S. and European domestic support** (internal/qualitative), and **global perceptions** (external/qualitative). For maximum effect, the resulting assessment should be placed against the backdrop of total dollars spent, and where possible, specific metrics should reflect both a numerical value and a percent increase or decrease from the previous year (or other logical baseline) to demonstrate a trend line. For the purposes of this report, the specific metrics offered for consideration in each category have been tailored to those most relevant to U.S. Army activities in Eastern and Central Europe.

Figure 1: Matrix for Evaluating Strategic Impact

	Internal	External
Quantitative	**U.S. and Allied Actions (A)**	**Russian Responses (B)**
Qualitative	**U.S. and European Domestic Support (C)**	**Global Perceptions (D)**

U.S. and Allied Actions

The category of "U.S. and allied actions" should include metrics that reflect tangible and direct U.S. and allied contributions to reassurance and deterrence efforts. ERI, a centerpiece of the U.S. response to Russia's aggressive actions, was designed to both assure and deter across five lines of effort: presence, training and exercises, prepositioned equipment, infrastructure, and building partner capacity. ERI was Washington's contribution to NATO's Readiness Action Plan (RAP) as well as its contribution of enablers to the VJTF. Demonstrable progress in these areas will resonate with policymakers and legislators by ensuring consistency and compliance with original intent as well as a demonstration of effective European burden sharing. Input metrics in this category could therefore include the following:

- *U.S. and allied troops in theater:* The number of U.S. troops in theater (shown as both a numeric value and a percent increase) is the key figure for measuring increased presence, and one that many European allies, rightly or wrongly, will look to in determining the degree of U.S. commitment to European security. The 2012 decision to reduce "legacy" U.S. forces stationed in Europe from four to two heavy BCTs continues to be a sensitive topic, particularly among NATO's eastern members who worry about the viability of NATO's Article 5 security guarantee. The ongoing EIC and the Army's Aviation Restructuring Initiative (ARI) have fueled similar concerns. For European allies, the sum total of both permanent and rotational U.S. ground forces will continue to matter. Citing the numerical and percent increase in planes and ships in theater, as well, will be a useful demonstration of the increased air, land, and sea presence promised by ERI. Enhancing contributions from all 28 allies will be key to demonstrating unity of effort and burden-sharing.

- *Allied troops in theater:* VJTF contribution, host-nation support, increase in defense spending, etc.

- *Training and exercises:* An increase in the size and frequency of training events and exercises in Europe, both those sponsored by USAREUR or those participated in by U.S. forces, will be another important and easily captured measure to show an increased commitment to building the capacity of U.S. allies and partners. A useful subcomponent of this metric may be the increase in training events and exercises specifically occurring in Eastern and Central Europe as well as NATO allies' participation and force contribution.

- *Prepositioned equipment:* EAS for exercises and training and APS to fulfill war plan requirements add significant credibility to assurance and deterrence efforts. Within these figures, it will be important to highlight the totals related to specific and recognizable capabilities that carry psychological weight with both with European and American audiences, such as the number of tanks and amount of ammunition.

- *Infrastructure improvements:* The metric for infrastructure improvements could range from the number of locations where projects are completed or underway, to specific projects such as the number of airstrips extended or built. The most compelling and insightful metrics will be those that capture the vast majority of spending in the fewest easily digestible buckets, while also making clear the benefit of infrastructure improvements to both allies and the United States. In addition, it would be useful to understand the level of Allied and host-nation support contributions.

- *Security assistance:* While the majority of change in this category may be best reflected by Foreign Military Financing (FMF) spending, DoD-specific investments may be captured via an increase in Section 1206/2282 activities in frontline states.

- *Indications and warnings:* These metrics relate to the time it takes for the United States to detect major movements of Russian military forces as well as detect internal political and economic dynamics and information operations that could be destabilizing, and then to provide that information to key decisionmakers. Ideally, U.S. forces will be able to gain as much advance warning as possible. In addition, it might be useful to understand the degree to which NATO allies integrated their intelligence and bilateral cyber capabilities.

Other metrics in this category could include:

- Total dollars spent by the United States and allies;

- Senior U.S. and European leader engagements and visits with counterparts;

- Implementation of lessons learned from regional and tabletop exercises;

- Defense and contingency plans revised or drafted; and

- Enhancements to command and control and interoperability.

Russian Responses

The category of "Russian responses" should include metrics that reflect quantifiable changes in Russian military operations and posture, doctrine, or behavior. While the causality of such changes will be difficult to conclusively determine, any notable changes to the security situation in the Baltic States and Central and Eastern Europe, especially those that are a priority for the United States, should be captured.

- Russian border incursions and military build-up, enhanced A2/AD capabilities, number and size of exercises, exercises with nuclear weapons, and increased treaty violations. Russia's increased presence and aggressive posture along its border with Europe has led to probing incursions of allied territory by land, air, and sea. The trend line associated with these types of events over time could be a useful measure of Russia's intentions. A caveat when using this statistic is the potential for skewed data given increases in U.S. and NATO ISR.

- Russian snap exercises without notification and violations of air and maritime space. Similar to border incursions, snap exercises are considered a visible, and much-discussed, sign of Russian saber-rattling and are therefore important to track. A noticeable uptick or decline could be indicative of the level of tensions in the region.

Other metrics in this category could include changes in the following:

- Estimated defense spending and quality of modernization;

- Changes to force deployments or basing;

- Training regimen or exercise schedule;

- Force structure or overall size of military;

- Weapons development or fielding plans;

- Russian military doctrine;

- Nature and frequency of public statements by senior government officials regarding defense and nuclear measures;

- Tone and content of academic and semi-government analyses and publications;

- Level of engagement with regional allies;

- Frequency or intensity of weapons testing;

- Based on open-source information, measures of success of information operations and negative change in public opinion toward NATO in allied countries; and

- Nature and frequency of defense messaging to Russian populace.

Domestic Support

The category of U.S. and allied "domestic support" should include metrics that reflect qualitative indications of the intangible costs and benefits of assurance and deterrence measures.

- *Political and domestic support in the United States and NATO countries:* In general, the long-term success and sustainability of military deployments is related to the amount of popular and political support the mission enjoys. A mission that is not well-understood, or is actively opposed, by the public can create a divisive political environment that makes funding and authorities more difficult to generate. Demonstrating public support for the assurance and deterrence mission or, at a minimum, avoiding strong opposition will be useful to highlight in conversations with congressional and parliamentary leaders.

- *Impact on U.S. and NATO forces:* Assessing the overall impact to the force may usefully call attention to the ancillary benefits of an increase in training and exercise deployments to building the readiness of U.S. forces, enhance territorial and collective defense measures, develop greater alliance interoperability, and regain European and Russian expertise that may have been lost after the Cold War. Confirmation that expanded rotational deployments do not impact U.S. troop dwell times or create new force health issues will help assuage concerns regarding over-commitment.

- *Ensuring NATO's continued relevance and returning NATO as a key pillar of U.S. national security:* While NATO's tasks are broader than Article 5 operations today, collective defense responsibilities have become an essential alliance task, returning NATO to its founding origins as a political-military organization dedicated to defending the territorial integrity of its members. Eroding and ultimately undermining NATO's credibility is one of the key objectives of the Kremlin. Should NATO assurance and deterrence mission vis-à-vis Russia fail, NATO would cease to exist as a relevant and valued alliance.

- *Security of the homeland:* Related to public support, demonstrating that the homeland is more, not less, secure because of a military deployment is essential to justifying the prioritization of missions with domestic audiences.

- *Threat prioritization and opportunity costs:* In terms of mission opportunity costs, policymakers might find it difficult to support additional deployments to Eastern Europe at the expense of reinforcements necessary to counter the Islamic State, for example. It will be important to make clear what, if any, anticipated impact an increased number of USAREUR forces would reasonably be expected to have on support to other missions, such as combatting the Islamic State. In terms of financial opportunity costs, the assurance and deterrence mission is indeed siphoning funds away from other military or domestic programs, but the mission is ultimately much cheaper than going to war with Russia, which will be a key point for budget discussions.

Global Perceptions

The category of "global perceptions" should include metrics that capture the qualitative impacts of assurance and deterrence measures on foreign audiences, including non-NATO allies, partners, and adversaries. Many of the below considerations require factoring in the consequences of inaction.

- *Demonstrating global U.S. leadership:* Ensuring that the United States continues to be perceived as a global leader is critical to all aspects of U.S. foreign policy, including our ability to build coalitions, credibly deter adversaries, and safeguard strategic stability. While the assurance and deterrence mission is not the sole linchpin upholding the United States' reputation as a global leader, the absence of U.S. action in this case would be widely perceived as an abdication of American leadership and would be antagonistic to U.S. interests in remaining a global leader.

- *Reinforcing the U.S. image as a dependable ally and partner:* The United States also has an interest in continuing to be perceived as a dependable ally and partner. If the majority of allies were to begin viewing the United States as undependable, they would be less likely to reciprocate support to both the United States and each other.

- *Pressuring European nations to maintain unity of effort with commensurate contributions:* The United States regularly takes the lead in contributing to operations and helps to set an expectation for commensurate contributions by all allies. Sustaining contributions from all 28 allies will be key to demonstrating unity of effort and burden-sharing, along with sending a message to Russia that NATO is resolute in its defense of the Baltic States. If the United States were to pull out of reassurance and deterrence operations, it is likely that the current alliance-wide effort would begin to crumble and Russia would be seen as gaining a victory for its attempt to undermine European cohesion.

- *Ensuring NATO's continued relevance:* While its core tasks are broader than Article 5 operations today, NATO was originally founded as a political-military organization dedicated to defending the territorial integrity of its members. The context of the assurance and deterrence mission vis-à-vis Russia is such that if NATO did not respond, many would questions the organization's continued relevance and value.

Other metrics in this category could include changes in the following:

- Allied readiness, interoperability, and capabilities; and

- Level of European anxiety

In summary, policymakers must keep in mind the inherent obstacles in quantitative assessments of influence strategies when attempting to capture the strategic impacts of U.S. reassurance and deterrence efforts in Central and Eastern Europe. Whether these measures are sustained or even expanded will depend on the combination of the results of the preceding impact assessment; the ability to effectively communicate the impact to Russia and other audiences; and a determination of whether continued or increased action remain within the United States' level of acceptable risk, which itself is somewhat unpredictable given the elusive line between deterrence and provocation. While imperfect, the use of a defined formula and systemic approach to measuring the impact of our efforts will help structure discussions, especially with the U.S. Congress, and provide greater visibility for a wider range of stakeholders.

Conclusions and Policy Recommendations

Specific budget recommendations to support an increased USAREUR deterrence posture in Europe are summarized below across the previously mentioned categories of prepositioned equipment; troop presence and personnel; and other critical capabilities needed to counter Russian forces.

Prepositioned Equipment

Sustain European Activity Set for a Rotational Armored Brigade Combat Team (sustain from FY16)

- Provides funding to sustain the European Activity Set (EAS) in FY16, which provides forward-deployed equipment for one rotational Armored Brigade Combat Team (ABCT).

New European Activity Set for a Second Rotational Armored Brigade Combat Team (new in FY17)

- Provides funding to establish a second EAS to provide forward-deployed equipment for a second rotational ABCT.

Enhanced European Activity Set for Rotational Enabler Forces (new in FY17)

- Provides funding for an EAS of enabling equipment that would include artillery, short-range air defense, engineers, heavy equipment transport, military police, military intelligence, sustainment, and signal equipment.

Army Prepositioned Stocks for Four Brigades (new in FY17)

- Building on the work in FY16, provides funding for equipment and supporting infrastructure for Army Prepositioned Stocks (APS) to support four brigades: two ABCTs, one sustainment brigade, and one fires brigade. Enhancing these stockpiles of equipment enables the United States to reduce time and transportation costs to provide armored forces for future exercises or contingencies.

Troop Presence and Personnel

Sustain Rotational Armored Brigade Combat Team Presence (sustain from FY16)

- Provides funding for a rotational Armored Brigade Combat Team (ABCT) through the rotation of the Regionally Aligned Force. During its approximate six-month rotations to Europe, this ABCT utilizes equipment from the European Activity Set (EAS) funded in FY16.

<u>Additional Rotational Armored Brigade Combat Team Presence</u> (new in FY17)

- Provides funding for a second rotational ABCT from the total force, providing a persistent presence of an ABCT in Europe. During its approximate six-month rotation, this ABCT would utilize equipment from the EAS funded in FY17.

<u>Enabling Headquarters Support</u> (new in FY17)

- Provides funding for a modest increase (approximately 1,000 personnel) in permanently assigned headquarters personnel to USAREUR to provide critical command-and-control capabilities for warfighting and to manage the increased tempo of rotational deployments.

- Provides funding for a 90-man Tactical Command Post (TAC), likely sourced from the 4th Infantry Division, to forward deploy to Europe to provide sufficient planning and execution capability for additional rotational forces.

- Provides funding for a permanently deployed composite fires brigade or division artillery headquarters, with a military intelligence company and an air and missile defense section to provide critical command-and-control capabilities for enabling forces.

- Provides funding for an increase in assigned personnel to USAREUR headquarters to enable it to serve as a Combined/Joint Forces Land Component Command (C/JFLCC). The C/JFLCC is a critical capability for planning and executing a joint and coalition ground war in Europe.

Capabilities

<u>Enhanced Logistics Capability</u> (new in FY17)

- Funds new logistics capabilities to support USAREUR forces and missions including additional assigned forces for the 21st Theater Sustainment Command, sufficient numbers of assigned heavy equipment transports operable in Europe, and bridging capability in order to properly set the theater and ensure adequate mobility for allocated and assigned U.S. forces.

<u>Infrastructure Improvements to Support Warm Basing</u> (sustain from FY16)

- Supports rotating forces to allied and partner bases in Eastern and Central Europe that do not regularly host U.S. forces including Novo Selo Training Area (NSTA) in Bulgaria and Mihail Kogalniceanu (MK) Air Base in Romania.

- Provides for basic infrastructure and logistical improvements to bases hosting rotational forces to better accommodate more frequent rotations and to demonstrate surge potential in the event of crises or contingencies.

<u>Increased Range Capacities</u> (sustain from FY16)

- Funds the necessary training to enable the joint reception, staging, onward movement, and integration (JRSOI) of training forces and ensures that adequate life support is provided for expeditionary U.S. forces.

Indications and Warnings (increase from FY16)

- Funds the retention of intelligence capabilities that provide shared immediate and mid-range indications and warning (I&W) capacity, all-source analysis, and open-source information awareness in support of operations, exercises, and training in the USEUCOM area of responsibility.

- Expands I&W capabilities related to hybrid threats, for example, increased monitoring of open-source information.

Cyber Capabilities (increase from FY16)

- Fields measures that better exploit Russian vulnerabilities and build allied resilience.

- Expands capacity for collaboration with the NATO Cooperative Cyber Defence Centre of Excellence located in Estonia.

- Conduct training scenarios for allies in a contested cyber domain.

Integrated Air and Missile Defense (IAMD) Capabilities (increase from FY16)

- Explores rotational deployments of Patriot systems and crews to Eastern and Central Europe.

Electronic Warfare Capabilities (increase from FY16)

- Increases electronic warfare capabilities to deny, disrupt, and defeat Russian manned and unmanned teamed systems, missile and radar vulnerabilities, as well as satellite-reliant systems.

- Funds the integration of EW systems into allied training and exercises.

Short Range Air Defense (SHORAD) (increase from FY16)

- Funds the increase of National Guard Avenger weapon-capable units' participation in NATO exercises.

Communications (increase from FY16)

- Fields additional secure, redundant, reliable communications with sufficient bandwidth.

- Funds enhancements to coalition tactical communications, coalition digital communications, and an unclassified common operating picture.

The CSIS study team believes the preceding elements are essential to a credible deterrence strategy for the U.S. Army in Europe. Note, however, that credible deterrence threats cannot prevent or completely alleviate the threat of coercive action by Russia. Even when deterrence succeeds in preventing war, a determined adversary can still design around deterrent threats to reach its objectives. Therefore, in the modern-day context of the Baltic States, policymakers must be prepared for lower-level Russian coercion that is not easily countered with traditional military means. Phase II of this study will assess the longer-term implications of Russia's new strategic posture for USAREUR for the next decade and consider how Russia may respond to various U.S. postures and actions.

About the Authors

Kathleen H. Hicks is senior vice president, Henry A. Kissinger Chair, and director of the International Security Program at CSIS. She is a frequent writer and lecturer on U.S. foreign and security policy; defense strategy, forces, and budget; and strategic futures. From 2009 to 2013, Dr. Hicks served as a senior civilian official in the Department of Defense. Confirmed in 2012 as principal deputy undersecretary of defense for policy, she was responsible for advising the secretary of defense on global and regional defense policy and strategy pertaining to such areas as the Asia-Pacific and Persian Gulf regions, Syria, and Europe. She also served as deputy undersecretary of defense for strategy, plans, and forces, leading the development of the 2012 Defense Strategic Guidance and the 2010 Quadrennial Defense Review and crafting guidance for future force capabilities, overseas military posture, and contingency and theater campaign plans.

From 2006 to early 2009, Dr. Hicks served as a senior fellow at CSIS, leading a variety of research projects in the national security field. From 1993 to 2006, she was a career civil servant in the Office of the Secretary of Defense, serving in a variety of capacities and rising from Presidential Management Intern to the Senior Executive Service. Dr. Hicks received numerous recognitions for her service in the Department of Defense (DoD), including distinguished awards from three secretaries of defense and the chairman of the Joint Chiefs of Staff. She also received the 2011 DoD Senior Professional Women's Association Excellence in Leadership Award. She holds a Ph.D. in political science from the Massachusetts Institute of Technology, an M.A. from the University of Maryland's School of Public Affairs, and an A.B. magna cum laude and Phi Beta Kappa from Mount Holyoke College. Dr. Hicks is an adjunct with the RAND Corporation and a member of the Council on Foreign Relations. She currently serves on the National Commission on the Future of the Army, the Board of Advisors for the Truman National Security Project, and the Board of Advisors for SoldierSocks, a veterans' charity.

Heather A. Conley is senior vice president for Europe, Eurasia, and the Arctic and director of the Europe Program at CSIS. Prior to joining CSIS in 2009, she served as executive director of the Office of the Chairman of the Board at the American National Red Cross. From 2001 to 2005, she served as deputy assistant secretary of state in the Bureau for European and Eurasian Affairs with responsibilities for U.S. bilateral relations with the countries of northern and central Europe. From 1994 to 2001, she was a senior associate with an international consulting firm led by former U.S. deputy secretary of state Richard L. Armitage. Ms. Conley began her career in the Bureau of Political-Military Affairs at the U.S. Department of State. She was selected to serve as special assistant to the coordinator of U.S. assistance to the newly independent states of the former Soviet Union. Ms. Conley is a member of the World Economic Forum's Global Agenda Council on the Arctic and is frequently featured as a foreign policy analyst on CNN, MSNBC, BBC, NPR, and PBS. She received her B.A. in international studies from West Virginia Wesleyan College and her M.A. in international relations from the Johns Hopkins University School of Advanced International Studies (SAIS).

Lisa Sawyer Samp is a fellow in the International Security Program at the Center for Strategic and International Studies (CSIS), where she focuses on defense strategy and European security. Her research areas include NATO, Europe/Russia, security cooperation, conventional and hybrid warfare, and defense posture. Prior to joining CSIS, Ms. Samp served on the National Security Council staff as director for NATO and European strategic affairs from 2014 to 2015, where she coordinated U.S. policy in preparation for the NATO Summit in Wales and managed the development of plans and force posture assessments to bolster alliance readiness and reassure allies following Russia's aggressive actions in Ukraine. Before and after her time at the White House, she worked as chief of staff to the assistant secretary of defense for international security affairs, advising on a range of issues related to U.S. defense policy in the Middle East, Europe, Russia/Ukraine/Eurasia, Africa, and the Western Hemisphere. While at the Pentagon, she also held the positions of NATO policy adviser and director for North Africa in the Office of the Secretary of Defense, supporting the full range of defense policy activities related to the 2011 military intervention in Libya. Ms. Samp joined the Department of Defense as a Presidential Management Fellow, serving at International Security Assistance Force (ISAF) headquarters in Kabul and at NATO headquarters in Brussels, among other assignments. She is a magna cum laude graduate of Baylor University with a B.A. in international studies and holds a M.A. in international affairs and development from George Washington University.

Olga Oliker is a senior adviser and director of the Russia and Eurasia Program at CSIS. Her recent research has focused on military, political, economic, and social development in countries in transition, particularly in Russia, Ukraine, and the Central Asian and Caucasian successor states to the Soviet Union. Prior to joining CSIS, Oliker held a number of senior posts at the RAND Corporation, most recently as director of RAND's Center for Russia and Eurasia. She is the author or coauthor of "Russian Foreign Policy in Historical and Current Context: A Reassessment" (*RAND Perspectives, 2015*), *Building Afghanistan's Security Forces in Wartime: The Soviet Experience* (RAND, 2011), *Nuclear Deterrence in Europe: Russian Approaches to a New Environment and Implications for the United States* (RAND, 2011), and *Russian Foreign Policy: Sources and Implications* (RAND, 2000), among other books, articles, and reports. She has also published commentary on Russia-related topics in print and online with the *New York Times, Chicago Tribune*, CNN, *U.S. News and World Report*, among others. Oliker holds a B.A. in international studies from Emory University and an M.P.P. from the Kennedy School of Government at Harvard University.

COL John A. O'Grady is currently serving as a military fellow at CSIS. Colonel O'Grady was commissioned as a field artillery officer upon his graduation from the U.S. Military Academy in 1990. He has held every key leadership position in the Field Artillery from platoon leader to most recently division artillery (DIVARTY) commander. His duty assignments include platoon leader, aide-de-camp, battalion S1, operations officer, battalion fire support officer, firing battery commander, fire support observer/controller (O/C) and senior fire support, battalion and DIVARTY S3, field artillery assignment officer, executive officer to the director, Officer Personnel Management Directorate (OPMD), battalion commander, and DIVARTY commander. Colonel O'Grady has been stationed stateside at Fort Hood, TX; Fort Sill, OK; and Alexandria, VA, and had multiple overseas assignments in Germany. His operational deployments consist of tours in both Iraq and Afghanistan. He has attended numerous military schools to include the Field Artillery Officer Basic and Advanced Course, Marine Amphibious Warfare School, Joint Firepower Control Course, Command and General Staff College, and the Dwight D. Eisenhower School for National Security. Colonel O'Grady's awards and decorations include Legion of Merit, Bronze Star Medal (1 OLC), Meritorious Service Medal (4 OLC), Army Commendation Medal (1 OLC), Army Achievement Medal (3 OLC), Global War on Terrorism Service and Expeditionary Medals, Afghanistan and Iraq Campaign Medals, the NATO medal, Combat Action Badge, and Parachutist Badge. Colonel O'Grady holds a bachelor's degree in leadership development from West Point, a master's in international management from Touro University in New York, and a master's in national resource strategy from the Eisenhower School for National Security at the National Defense University.

Jeffrey Rathke is a senior fellow and the deputy director of the CSIS Europe Program. Prior to his current position, Mr. Rathke served as the director of the State Department Press Office from May 2014 to June 2015 (and acting deputy spokesperson in April and May). He joined the Foreign Service in 1991 and retired in June 2015. During his Foreign Service tenure, Mr. Rathke served as deputy director of the Private Office of the NATO secretary general in Brussels (2009–2011) and as minister-counselor for political affairs (2006–2009) at the U.S. Embassy in Berlin. His Washington assignments include deputy director of the Office of European Security and Political Affairs (EUR/RPM) and as a duty officer in the White House Situation Room and the State Department Operations Center. Mr. Rathke was a Weinberg Fellow at Princeton University from 2003–2004, winning the Master's in Public Policy Prize. He served at the U.S. Embassy in Dublin from 2001–2003, covering multilateral politics during Ireland's tenure on the UN Security Council. From 1999–2001, Mr. Rathke was posted in Moscow and was responsible for relations with the Russian legislative branch in the Political Section. Mr. Rathke was assigned to the U.S. Embassy Office in Berlin from 1994–1996 and helped open the U.S. Embassy in Riga from 1992–1994. Jeff Rathke has been awarded several Superior Honor and Meritorious Honor Awards. He holds a master's degree in public policy from Princeton University and B.A. and B.S. degrees from Cornell University. He speaks German, Russian, and Latvian.

Melissa Dalton is a fellow and the chief of staff of the CSIS International Security Program (ISP). Her research focuses on security cooperation, U.S. defense policy in the Middle East, and defense strategy and policy. As chief of staff, she advises the director of ISP on a broad range of strategic and management issues. She joined CSIS in 2014 as a visiting fellow in ISP and as a 2014–2015 Council on Foreign Relations international affairs fellow. Prior to CSIS, she served in a number of positions at the U.S. Department of Defense (DoD), in the Office of the Under Secretary of Defense for Policy from 2007 to 2014. Most recently, she was a senior adviser for force planning. Previously, she served as special assistant to the undersecretary of defense for policy, as policy adviser to the commander of the International Security Assistance Force in Kabul, Afghanistan, and as country director for Lebanon and Syria. In 2012, she was a visiting fellow at the Center for a New American Security. Prior to her DoD service, she taught English to middle and high school students in Damascus, Syria, in 2006. From 2003 to 2005, she served as an intelligence analyst at the Defense Intelligence Agency. She holds a B.A. in foreign affairs from the University of Virginia and an M.A. in international relations and international economics from the Johns Hopkins University School of Advanced International Studies. She is a term member in the Council on Foreign Relations.

Anthony Bell is a research associate with the International Security Program at CSIS, where he works on a broad range of U.S. defense and security policy issues related to Europe and the Middle East. Prior to joining CSIS, he worked with the Office of the Secretary of Defense on counterterrorism and security issues in Libya and North Africa. He previously worked as a research assistant at the Institute for the Study of War focusing on political and security dynamics in Iraq, Afghanistan, and Libya. Since 2013, he has served as an instructional assistant at the George Washington University for courses on foreign policy decisionmaking and international security politics. Mr. Bell graduated magna cum laude and Phi Beta Kappa from the George Washington University with a B.A. in international affairs and received his M.A. in security studies from Georgetown University.

www.ingramcontent.com/pod-product-compliance
Lightning Source LLC
Chambersburg PA
CBHW081437270326
41932CB00019B/3247

* 9 7 8 1 4 4 2 2 5 9 2 4 9 *